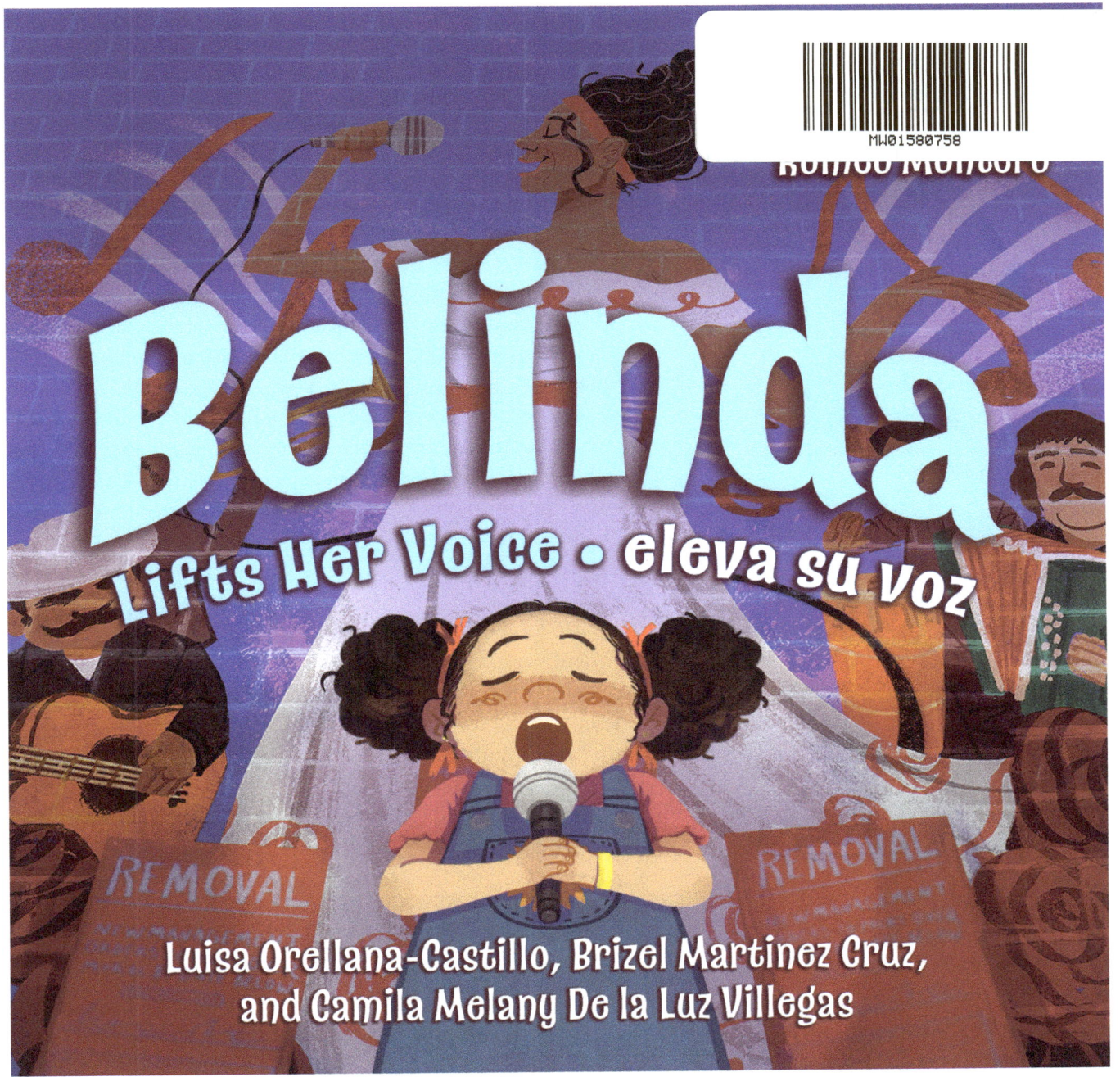

Belinda
Lifts Her Voice • eleva su voz

Luisa Orellana-Castillo, Brizel Martinez Cruz, and Camila Melany De la Luz Villegas

Latin American Youth Center | Washington, DC
Shout Mouse Press

**Latin American Youth Center/
Shout Mouse Press**

Text copyright © 2023 by
Shout Mouse Press

Illustrations copyright © 2023
by Romeo Montero

Design by Amber Colleran

Spanish translation by
Isabel C. Mendoza

ISBN: 978-1-950807-64-2

SHOUT MOUSE PRESS

Shout Mouse Press is a nonprofit writing and publishing program dedicated to amplifying underheard voices. Learn more and see our full catalog at www.shoutmousepress.org.

Shout Mouse Press
1638 R Street NW Suite 218
Washington, DC 20009

Trade distribution:
Ingram Book Group

For information about special discounts and bulk purchases, please contact Shout Mouse Press sales at 240-772-1545 or orders@shoutmousepress.org.

Shout Mouse Press supports copyright. Copyright fuels creativity, encourages diverse voices, promotes free speech, and creates a vibrant culture. Thank you for buying an authorized edition of this book and for complying with copyright laws by not reproducing, scanning, or distributing any part of it in any form without permission. You are supporting writers and allowing Shout Mouse to continue to publish books for every reader.

Acknowledgments

At Shout Mouse Press, we invite young people to write diverse and inclusive stories inspired by their own lived experiences. We believe that all children should be able to see themselves in the books they read, and that all children benefit from reading diverse perspectives on our shared world.

This book, written by young people from the Latin American Youth Center in Washington, DC, is born of this mission. These youth authors, ages 16-22, worked in teams of three to compose original children's books centering the stories of immigrant families. They put their own hearts—and their personalities!—on the page, writing stories they hoped would inspire young readers to embrace who they are and to value the unique stories each one of us has to tell. These authors have our immense gratitude and respect: Melany, Brizel, Luisa, Sol, Jonathan, Yasmina, Yenner, Mich, and Jonatan.

This project represents a collaboration between Shout Mouse Press and the Latin American Youth Center (LAYC). From LAYC: Thanks to Cheili Obregon-Molina, Kamila Rivera Diaz, Elizabeth Silva, and Yazmyn Aguilar for essential translation, collaboration, and positive energy, and to the program leadership of Marie Moll Amego. From Shout Mouse Press: We thank Programs Director Alexa Patrick and Programs Coordinator Carlynn Newhouse as well as Story Coaches Faith Campbell, Tatiana Figueroa Ramirez, and Chelsea Iorlano for making workshops fun, productive, and supportive for these young writers. We can't thank enough illustrators Yurieli Otero-Asmar, Romeo Montero, and Hee So for bringing these stories to life with their beautiful artwork, and Amber Colleran for bringing a keen eye and important mentorship to the project as the series Art Director. Also muchísimas gracias are in order for Isabel C. Mendoza for her thoughtful translation. We are grateful for the time and talents of all of these writers, mentors, and artists!

Finally, this project was made possible by funding from the National Endowment for the Arts, the DC Commission on the Arts and Humanities, and EventsDC. Thank you!

To those who have lost loved ones—this book is for you.
Your loved ones are always cheering you on. May you
honor their legacy and cherish their memories.

Para quienes han perdido a seres queridos: este libro es
para ustedes. Sus seres queridos siempre están alentándolos.
Honren su legado y mantengan vivo su recuerdo.

When Papá and I are in the car, he always plays our music: bachata, rancheras, banda…
 …and I always sing along.

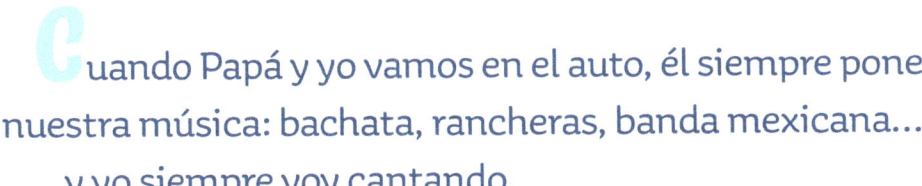

Cuando Papá y yo vamos en el auto, él siempre pone nuestra música: bachata, rancheras, banda mexicana…
 …y yo siempre voy cantando.

"*¡Y volver, volver, volver!*"

"Ah, Tía's favorite song," Papá says fondly.

I know he misses her. Almost as much as I do.

"Your voice is beautiful, mijita, just like hers. Why did you stop sharing it?"

But I don't answer... I just sigh, and look out the window.

«¡Y volver, volver, volver!».

—Ah, la canción favorita de la tía —dice Papá con cariño.

Sé que él la extraña. Tanto como yo.

—Tú tienes una linda voz, mijita; como la de ella. ¿Por qué no volviste a cantar?

Yo no respondo nada... Solo suspiro, y miro por la ventana.

Finally, we turn onto Abuela's street. We pass vendors selling my favorite drinks—horchata and agua de jamaica—and squeezing lemon over mangoes. Mmmmm.

Por fin, llegamos a la calle donde vive la abuela. Pasamos frente a unas personas que están vendiendo mis bebidas favoritas (horchata y agua de jamaica) y exprimiendo limón sobre unos mangos. Mmmmm.

Just ahead, I see my favorite part of the neighborhood: Tía's mural.

Más adelante, veo mi parte favorita del vecindario: el mural de mi tía.

My tía was like my second mother.

She was kind-hearted. She was funny. When she sang, people's troubles went away.

My troubles went away, too. When I sang with Tía, I felt so happy! I felt confident. I felt like *anything* was possible.

So when we lost her, I felt like I lost... everything.

At least we still have her mural.

Mi tía era como mi segunda madre.

Era bondadosa. Era chistosa. La gente olvidaba sus problemas cuando la escuchaba cantar.

Yo también olvidaba los *míos*. ¡Me sentía muy feliz cuando cantaba con mi tía! Sentía confianza en mí misma. Como si *cualquier* cosa fuera posible.

Por eso, cuando la perdimos, sentí que había perdido... todo.

Por lo menos, todavía tenemos su mural.

But wait —

"Papá, why are there big red posters on Tía's mural?!"

Papá stops the car and reads the poster. His eyes grow wide.

"It says the city plans to remove the mural. A new restaurant is opening here."

"No! Why?! They can't do that!!" I cry out.

"There must be something we can do," Papá says.

¡Un momento!

—Papá, ¡¿qué hacen esos enormes carteles rojos el mural de la tía?!

Papá detiene el auto y lee el cartel. Sus ojos se abren como platos.

—Dice que la ciudad planea quitar el mural. Aquí van a poner un restaurante nuevo.

—¡No! ¡¿Por qué?! ¡No pueden hacer eso! —grito.

—Tiene que haber algo que podamos hacer para impedirlo —dice Papá.

When we arrive at Abuela's, we learn that the news of the red poster has spread quickly. Our family already knows. No one can believe it.

"We are planning a protest this weekend to save the mural," Tío Berto says. "We need to pass out these flyers. Will you help?"

"Of course!" I say.

Cuando llegamos donde la abuela, nos enterarse de que la noticia del cartel rojo se ha propagado rápidamente. Nuestra familia ya lo sabe. Nadie lo puede creer.

—Estamos organizando una protesta este fin de semana para salvar el mural —dice mi tío Berto—. Necesitamos repartir estos volantes. ¿Nos ayudan?

—¡Por supuesto! —digo yo.

My cousin Juan comes with Papá and me to give out flyers in the neighborhood.

But… lots of people don't even answer their doors. Others think we're trying to sell something and say, *No thanks!*

"What's the point?!" Juan complains. "No one's even listening!"

We sit in silence, but I know what my tía would say:

It's not always easy… Keep trying and never give up!

Mi primo Juan viene con Papá y conmigo a repartir los volantes por el vecindario.

Pero… mucha gente ni siquiera nos abre la puerta. Otros creen que les queremos vender algo, y nos dicen «¡No, gracias!».

—¡¿Qué sentido tiene todo esto?! —se queja Juan—. ¡Nadie nos escucha!

Nos sentamos en silencio; pero yo sé lo que diría mi tía:

«No siempre es fácil… Sigue intentándolo, ¡y nunca te rindas!».

We return to Abuela's house to make another plan.

"So, now what?" Papá asks. "How else can we bring people out to support?"

On the wall, I see a picture of my tía laughing at her last birthday party. This gives me an idea.

"Tía loved parties," I say. "What if we threw a *party* at the mural instead?"

Regresamos a la casa de la abuela para hacer otro plan.

—¿Y ahora, qué? —pregunta Papá—. ¿De qué otra manera podemos atraer gente para que nos apoye?

En la pared, veo un retrato de mi tía en su último cumpleaños, riéndose. Se me ocurre una idea.

—A mi tía le encantaban las fiestas —digo—. ¿Qué tal si más bien hacemos una *fiesta* en el mural?

Just then, the phone rings.

"Hello... Who is this?" Abuela asks. "Oh, a reporter! Well, plans have changed..."

She smiles at us. "It's not just a protest anymore," she tells the reporter. "It's a party."

En ese momento, suena el teléfono.

—Hola... ¿Quién habla? —responde la abuela—. ¡Oh, un reportero! Bueno, pues ha habido un cambio de planes...

La abuela nos sonríe.

—Ya no es tan solo una protesta —le dice al reportero—. Es una fiesta.

The day of the party is perfect—warm and sunny.

Abuela's tamales, horchata, and pupusas are all ready. The rancheras are playing loudly, and a crowd begins to gather.

Papá steps up onto the stage. "¡Bienvenidos todos! Get up and dance, get some food... Just make sure you leave some tamales for me!"

Everyone laughs and the party begins.

~

El día de la fiesta es perfecto: cálido y soleado.

Los tamales, la horchata y las pupusas de la abuela están listos. Suenan rancheras a todo volumen, y comienza a llegar la gente.

Papá sube al escenario.

—¡Bienvenidos todos! Bailen y coman... ¡Solo asegúrense de dejar algunos tamales para mí!

Todos se ríen, y comienza la fiesta.

Just then, a TV news van pulls up and a reporter and camera woman step out.

"It's an honor to be here to celebrate Tía Sofía," says the reporter into the camera. "Her music was inspiring to me and to the whole community."

One by one, people gather around the reporter, sharing their stories of how Tía Sofía inspired them, too.

Entonces, llega la camioneta de un noticiero de televisión, y de ella se bajan una reportera y una camarógrafa.

—Es un honor estar aquí, rindiendo un homenaje a la Tía Sofía —dice la reportera mirando a la cámara—. Su música me sirvió de inspiración a mí, y a toda la comunidad.

La gente se va congregando poco a poco alrededor de la reportera para compartir historias de cómo la Tía Sofía también inspiró a otros.

Suddenly, the music stops.

A man in a suit stands up on stage and yells, "This is private property now! You need to take your party somewhere else!"

"We are celebrating a great woman!" Papá calls out. "This mural honors her!" Other people in the crowd shout too.

De repente, se detiene la música.

Un hombre vestido de traje sube al escenario y grita:

—¡Este lugar ahora es propiedad privada! ¡Váyanse con su fiesta a otro lado!

—¡Estamos rindiendo un homenaje a una gran mujer! —grita Papá—. ¡Este mural se hizo en su honor!

Otra gente también grita.

With all the yelling, it doesn't feel like a party anymore. I look up at my beloved Tía on the wall, her chin held high as if nothing can stop her.
I think I know what to do.
Heart pounding, I walk toward the stage...

Con tantos gritos, esto ya no parece una fiesta. Yo miro el rostro de mi querida tía en la pared, con la frente en alto, como si nada pudiera detenerla.
«Creo que ya sé lo que debo hacer».
Con el corazón palpitándome a mil por hora, camino hacia el escenario...

I start to sing.

"*Y volver, volver, volver...*"

Everyone gets quiet. All eyes are on me. I freeze.

Silence.

But then... I hear Papá's voice, continuing the chorus. Then Abuela's. I close my eyes and keep singing, as more voices join in.

Comienzo a cantar.

«Y volver, volver, volver...».

Todo el mundo se calla. Todas las miradas se posan sobre mí. Yo me paralizo.

Silencio.

Pero, entonces... oigo la voz de Papá, cantando el coro. Luego, la de la abuela. Cierro los ojos y sigo cantando, mientras otras voces se unen.

When I open my eyes, the whole party is singing along. Even the man in the suit.
In my heart, a familiar voice rings through them all...

Cuando abro los ojos, todos los asistentes a la fiesta están cantando conmigo. Hasta el hombre del traje.
En medio de todas las voces, escucho en mi corazón una voz conocida...

Tía Sofía?

I smile and sing even louder.

¿Tía Sofía?

Sonrío, y canto más fuerte todavía.

About the Authors

Luisa Orellana-Castillo

I am a 15-year-old girl from Washington, DC, currently in the 9th grade. My mother is from El Salvador, and my father is from Bolivia. I have two siblings who I love deeply. I like to listen to many different types of music, especially when I study and play video games. When I wrote this book, I enjoyed having to connect through personal experiences with the people I collaborated with. I wrote this book not just to increase diversity in children's books, but also to show deep cultural significance. I hope readers can learn more about the cultures being expressed in this book!

Brizel Martinez Cruz

I am 15 years old and a sophomore in high school. I am also a first-generation American with Mexican parents, a little sister, and an adorable little dog. Some of my hobbies include baking, crocheting, and writing poems and short stories. This is my first published book. My favorite part of this writing process was collaborating with my team members and sharing our perspectives and personal experiences while deciding certain story elements. I hope readers enjoy this story which is meant to promote youth power, cultural diversity, and honoring lost loved ones.

Camila Melany De la Luz Villegas

I am a high school student in Washington, DC and a first-generation Mexican-American. I have a big family: four brothers, one sister, four amazing parents—my mom and step-dad and my dad and step-mom—three cats, and a husky. I like music and sports. My favorite part of working on this book was being able to connect with my team members, sharing laughs and jokes, and having our story come to life. I was able to honor my grandpa through writing this book. He was a great man and a father figure in my life. I chose to write this book because I wanted other kids to see themselves in the story the way that I couldn't growing up.

Chelsea Iorlano served as Story Coach for this book.

About the Authors

Luisa Orellana-Castillo

Soy una chica de 15 años de Washington D. C. y estoy en noveno grado. Mi madre es de El Salvador y mi padre es de Bolivia. Tengo dos hermanos a quienes quiero muchísimo. Me gusta escuchar diferentes tipos de música, especialmente cuando estudio y juego videojuegos. Durante el proceso de escribir este libro, disfruté el tener que conectarme a través de mis experiencias personales con los otros miembros del equipo. Escribí este libro no solo para ayudar a ampliar la diversidad en los libros infantiles, sino también para mostrar un sentido profundo de la cultura. ¡Espero que los lectores aprendan más acerca de las culturas que se representan en este libro!

Brizel Martinez Cruz

Tengo 15 años, y estoy en décimo grado. Soy mexicoamericana de primera generación, y tengo una hermana menor y un perrito hermoso. Entre mis pasatiempos están la repostería, tejer con ganchillo y escribir poemas y cuentos. Este es el primer libro que publico. Mi parte favorita del proceso de escritura fue trabajar con los otros miembros del equipo y compartir nuestras perspectivas y experiencias personales para tomar decisiones sobre ciertos elementos del cuento. Espero que los lectores disfruten esta historia, cuya intención es promover el poder de los jóvenes, la diversidad cultural y el homenaje a los seres queridos que se han marchado.

Camila Melany De la Luz Villegas

Soy estudiante de bachillerato en Washington D. C. y mexicoamericana de primera generación. Tengo una familia grande: cuatro hermanos, una hermana, cuatro padres maravillosos (mi madre y mi padrastro, y mi padre y mi madrastra), tres gatos y un perro esquimal. Me gustan la música y los deportes. Mi parte favorita del proceso de escribir este libro fue el poder conectar con los otros miembros del equipo, compartir risas y chistes, y darle vida a nuestro cuento. A través de la escritura de este libro, pude rendir un homenaje a mi abuelo, quien fue un gran hombre y una figura paterna para mí. Elegí escribir este libro porque quería que otros chicos se vieran reflejados en una historia; una oportunidad que yo de niña no tuve.

About the Illustrator

Romeo Montero

My name is Romeo Montero and I am an illustrator attending Moore College of Art & Design. I love creating vibrant and dynamic illustrations. My work is heavy in texture, goats, nature, and anything else I personally find cool. I am committed to anti-racist and anti-colonial praxis, and use my art as a way of exploring new worlds, possibilities, and as a vessel to heal myself and my community. When I'm not drawing, you can find me at a metal show headbanging the night away. You can find more of my work here: https://fmontero.myportfolio.com

Romeo Montero

Me llamo Romeo Montero, soy ilustrador y actualmente tomo clases en Moore College of Art & Design. Me encanta crear ilustraciones vibrantes y dinámicas. Mis obras están repletas de texturas, cabras, naturaleza y cualquier otra cosa que me pueda parecer interesante. Estoy comprometido con las prácticas anti-racistas y anti-colonialistas, y uso mi arte para explorar nuevos mundos y posibilidades, y como un vehículo para sanarme a mí mismo y a mi comunidad. Cuando no estoy dibujando, me puedes encontrar "cabeceando" en un concierto de metal. Aquí puedes ver otras obras mías: https://fmontero.myportfolio.com

Writers and artists at work

ABOUT LAYC

The Latin American Youth Center (LAYC) is a DC-based nonprofit organization that offers a variety of programming to low-income youth of all backgrounds. Their mission is to empower a diverse population of young people to achieve a successful transition to adulthood, through multicultural, comprehensive, and innovative programs that address youths' social, academic, and career needs.

El Latin American Youth Center (LAYC) es una organización sin fines de lucro con sede en Washington D. C. que ofrece una variedad de programas para jóvenes de bajos recursos de todos los orígenes. Su misión consiste en capacitar a una población diversa de jóvenes para que logren una transición exitosa a la edad adulta a través de programas multiculturales, integrales e innovadores que abordan las necesidades sociales, académicas y profesionales de la juventud.

Learn more at layc-dc.org

ABOUT SHOUT MOUSE PRESS

Shout Mouse Press is a nonprofit organization dedicated to centering and amplifying the voices of marginalized youth (ages 12+) via writing workshops, publication, and public speaking opportunities. The young people we coach are underrepresented—as characters and as creators—within young people's literature, and their perspectives underheard. Our work provides a platform for them to tell their own stories and, as published authors, to act as leaders and agents of change.

Shout Mouse Press es una organización sin fines de lucro dedicada a centrar y amplificar las voces de los jóvenes marginalizados (a partir de los 12 años) a través de talleres de escritura, publicación y oportunidades para hablar en público. La gente joven a la que entrenamos está subrepresentada —como personajes y como creadores— en la literatura para gente joven, y sus perspectivas son poco escuchadas. Nuestro trabajo les proporciona una plataforma para contar sus propias historias y, como autores publicados, actuar como líderes y agentes de cambio.

Learn more at shoutmousepress.org

MORE BOOKS FROM SHOUT MOUSE PRESS

Shout Mouse Press is passionate about letting young people speak for themselves—and making sure they are heard. We lead writing and art workshops that center youth voices, then edit and design their books, and finally publish and promote their important work. We ensure that earned income from book sales is invested directly back into young people themselves: proceeds support scholarship funds for author communities, salaries for author interns, and programs that help young people speak up, be heard, and be taken seriously as leaders in their community.

Check out our catalogue of 50+ award-winning youth-authored titles including children's books, graphic novels, novels, memoirs, and poetry collections at **shoutmousepress.org**.

   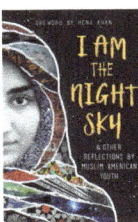 

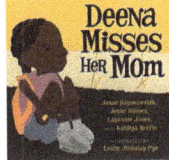 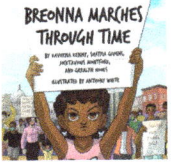 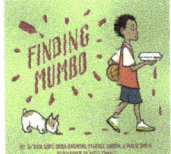 

WHERE TO BUY

We encourage you to order books directly through Shout Mouse Press online in order to best benefit our authors. For bulk orders, educator inquiries, and nonprofit discounts: email **orders@shoutmousepress.org**.

Books are also available through Amazon, Bookshop.org, and other online retailers.

Shout Mouse titles are distributed by Ingram.

OTHER WAYS TO ENGAGE

Shout Mouse Press can bring speakers to your class or event. Call us at 240-772-1545 or request via **shoutmousepress.org/request-an-author-talk**.

Support our youth writing and publishing programs by becoming a donor: **shoutmousepress.org/donate**.

OUR IMPACT

120,000+
Shout Mouse books in circulation

20+
Book Industry Honors, including 4 Book of the Year Designations

$200,000+
raised in scholarship funds for author communities

20,000+
audience members reached through 100+ Author Talks in schools, libraries, and conferences

20,000+
books donated to young readers in need

SHOUT MOUSE PRESS / LAYC BILINGUAL BOOK SPOTLIGHT:

VOCES SIN FRONTERAS

As immigrants and activists, the Latino Youth Leadership Council of LAYC recognized the urgent need for #OwnVoices stories to provide a human face to the U.S. immigration debate. With few youth-focused books reflecting their personal narratives, they decided to boldly share their own. The Shout Mouse team of teaching artists and comic coaches worked with these youth leaders to share their memoirs about immigrating to the U.S., and now educators across the country are using their stories to educate, affirm, and inspire their students. For ages 12+.

Voces Sin Fronteras: Our Stories, Our Truth
978-1945434921

Voces Sin Fronteras is a bilingual collection of 16 self-illustrated graphic memoirs by teen immigrants from Central America and the Caribbean. These thought-provoking and powerfully honest stories address themes of poverty, family, grief, education, and, of course, the pain and promise of immigration. This book is an opportunity to hear directly from youth who are often in the headlines but whose stories don't get told in full. Foreword by Newbery Medal winner Meg Medina.

"When I tell my story, it heals what it is in my past.... If you never share, the pain will never leave, it will always be there... [Telling your story] will help you to heal inside, to be who you are, to speak out."

— Erminia, co-author of *Voces Sin Fronteras*, on the power of sharing her story via Author Talks

REVIEWS

"This powerful compendium amplifies teens' understanding of the young immigrant experience— facing fears, overcoming sadness, learning a new language, and being left by parents who migrated first, then forgiving and reuniting with them decades later... VERDICT: Spotlighting underrepresented voices, this work is highly recommended for all communities in their efforts to promote empathetic, inclusive discussions around immigration."
—*School Library Journal*, Starred Review

"The compelling stories shared by these students… signal their desire to serve as beacons or lifelines for other young immigrants. Their testimonies, as Newbery Medal winner Meg Medina points out in her foreword, are ultimately about courage… Enlightening and inspiring #ownvoices accounts by young activists." — Kirkus Reviews

AWARDS

2020 International Latino Book Awards
Best Young Adult Nonfiction

2019 "In the Margins"
Top Nonfiction Prize